de Havilland MOSQUITO

INFO GUIDE Nº· 1

Welcome to the Plane Essentials *'InfoGuide No.1'*, which takes as its subject the world-famous de Havilland Mosquito. This monograph is the first in an important new series of publications on specific aircraft types that have been significant in the history of aviation, from the earliest times to the present day. In one straightforward reference source is the story of this renowned aircraft, backed up with illustrations that show the Mosquito in many of its successful roles and variants. The *InfoGuide* series aims to educate but at the same time stimulate interest in the aircraft types that are covered in the series, and act as an encouragement for further research and reading.

'Mosquito – InfoGuide No.1' tells the story of the famed and highly-versatile de Havilland D.H. 98 Mosquito twin-engined fighter-bomber, reconnaissance aircraft and night-fighter, and the vital roles that it played in World War Two for the British and Commonwealth aircrews who took this excellent aircraft to war. Individual chapters detail the type's development, operational service, and many other aspects of this highly significant warplane. Nicknamed the 'Wooden Wonder', the Mosquito was unique amongst major Second World War combat aircraft by including wood as a major part of its construction. It was one of the most important Allied warplanes of that conflict, and it also saw valuable service after World War Two for a number of air forces around the world.

Featuring contemporary photographs and the well-known artwork of John Batchelor, together with side-view illustrations from the similarly celebrated illustrator Mark Rolfe, *'Mosquito – InfoGuide No.1'* portrays the Mosquito in its many variants and sheds light on the diverse colour schemes worn by operational Mosquitoes. Informative illustrations show details such as cockpit interiors and equipment, while cutaway drawings demonstrate the Mosquito's inner features and its unique construction. A separate section lists manufacturers of scale models and accessories that are available to allow accurate replicas to be built of this important warplane. *'Mosquito – InfoGuide No.1'* is an affordable and detailed reference source for enthusiasts, historians and model-makers, and adds to the available published knowledge on this important British warplane.

Malcolm V. Lowe.

Published by Publishing Solutions (www) Ltd. in association with The Minster Press, Great Britain.

Acknowledgements - The Author and Illustrators gratefully acknowledge the assistance of a number of colleagues and contacts during the preparation of this title. They include Martin Hale, John Neale, Bob Richards, Ron Schneiter, Caroline Sheen (Photography and Illustrations Editor, 'Air & Space Smithsonian' magazine), Didier Waelkens (IPMS Belgium), and British Aerospace (now BAE Systems). Technical assistance was provided by former RAF Pathfinder Bill Burke. Particular thanks to the Author's Father, Victor Lowe, for proof-reading together with first-hand experience and assistance, and to Capt Eric 'Winkle' Brown for background material on RN Mosquitoes. Special thanks also to the staff of The Minster Press for their professional help with the creation of this book.

© 2008 Publishing Solutions (www) Ltd. www.publishingsolutionswww.com

Text: Malcolm Lowe
Illustrations: John Batchelor
1/72 Colour side views: Mark Rolfe and Malcolm Lowe
Production, typesetting and design: The Minster Press, The Old Church House, 5 Mill Lane, Wimborne Minster, Dorset, BH21 1JQ, Great Britain.
Tel. 01202 882277 www.printsolutions.co.uk

ISBN 978-1-906589-00-4

Contents

The 'Wooden Wonder'

From a log to a plane: strips of wood are peeled from the trunk and steamed to fit around the spars and moulds to form the inner skin. A central filling of balsa wood is subsequently added. The outer skin of plywood is then strapped down onto it. The two halves are then fitted out internally before being joined together to make the fuselage. The wings were made from similar material (Photos: HSA - Hawker Siddeley Aviation, successor to de Havilland).

Three Mosquito prototypes were built which pioneered production layouts and equipment fits. E0234 was the 'B' Condition serial originally allocated to the first of the Mosquito line. Better known as W4050, this aircraft first flew on 25 November 1940 (Photo: HSA).

Chapter 1 Development and Background

One of the finest warplanes of World War II was undoubtedly de Havilland's elegant and highly successful Mosquito. Conceived as a private-venture by a company not closely associated with high-performance warplane design and construction in the pre-war era, the Mosquito nevertheless went on to become a vital tool in the Allied aerial arsenal as the Second World War progressed. It was also one of the most versatile aircraft of World War II, performing a variety of roles including those of fighter-bomber, night-fighter, anti-shipping, reconnaissance and training. The Mosquito in a myriad of versions performed these significant tasks with great capability, operated by brave and sometimes celebrated RAF and Commonwealth aircrews who flew with distinction in the skies over Europe, the Mediterranean and the Far East. Most Mosquitoes were built in Britain by de Havilland and a number of sub-contractors, but production also took place in Canada and Australia by de Havilland's related companies. Eventually some 7,781 Mosquitoes of all types were built in over 40 distinct versions, with initial production aircraft being delivered in August 1941 and manufacture continuing until 1950. The type also served post-war with a variety of overseas air arms, the final Mosquitoes not being retired until the 1960's.

The Mosquito was virtually unique amongst the major warplanes of World War Two in being constructed principally from wood. In an age where the all-metal stressed-skin monoplane had become the accepted construction layout for most combat aircraft, the Mosquito instead harked back to an earlier age in its use of wood, albeit in the most advanced employment known at that time of this natural material. Wood had been used in the construction of aircraft during and since the dawn of manned powered flight, but during the 1930's it had been largely replaced for front-line combat aircraft by all-metal or predominantly all-metal structures. However, the de Havilland company had gained considerable experience in the creation of fast, wood construction twin-engined aircraft with the design of the famous D.H. 88 Comet racing aircraft of the early 1930's, which won the England to Australia air race of 1934. The company had also created the beautifully-streamlined pre-war Albatross airliner. Design of the Mosquito drew on these experiences, and commenced in 1938 as a private venture project. Although de Havilland's thinking in that direction had been prompted by the British Air Ministry's Specification P.13/36 for a new medium bomber, the company wanted to go further than this requirement and at first looked at bomber adaptations of existing designs such as the Albatross airliner. Eventually, however, a new design for a twin-engined wood-construction bomber was decided upon. It would be aerodynamically clean, and powered by the Rolls-Royce Merlin engine which even at that early time in the Merlin's service employment offered much promise. It was hoped that the new aircraft would additionally be fast enough to out-run enemy fighters – and therefore would not need defensive armament such as gun turrets or their gunners. This was a complete contradiction to contemporary established design philosophy. The new design eventually gained the in-house designation D.H. 98.

Prototype Development

Unfortunately the radical thinking that went behind the D.H. 98 project was almost its undoing. In October 1938 de Havilland put its case forward for the new design to the Air Ministry, albeit without success – it was too radical for the time. There were subsequently further studies and some informal talks but no progress could be made until Germany's invasion of Poland in September, 1939. The project was again put forward by de Havilland, and fortunately the interest of Air Marshal Sir Wilfrid Freeman, Air Member for Development and Production, was enlisted. In the weeks that followed the design was subjected to official study, and there was much discussion about the need for the addition of rear guns and a gunner. Nevertheless, at a conference on 29 December 1939, the company was authorised to proceed with the unarmed formula. The basic requirement was for a bomb load of 1,000 lb (454 kg), a range of 1,500 miles (2,414 km) - the sortie radius being half that distance - and the performance characteristics of a fighter. There was also equal interest on the Ministry side in a photographic reconnaissance version of the aircraft.

Design work duly commenced at a rapid pace. Much of this was performed at an old country house a few miles from de Havilland's main base at Hatfield, called Salisbury Hall. The design team was led by R. E. Bishop and the design itself was numbered as the D.H. 98, with the name "Mosquito" being adopted early in the programme. On 1 March 1940, de Havilland received a contract for 50 Mosquito bombers, including the prototype, straight off the drawing board and conforming to Specification B.1/40. However, just after the Dunkirk evacuation, Lord Beaverbrook was appointed Minister of Aircraft Production in the new Churchill Government - anxious to concentrate existing capacity on immediate operational needs, he deleted the B.1/40 from the programme. This held up work and made permission to buy materials much more difficult, but de Havilland managed in July to gain authorization to continue, provided work did not interfere with the production of Airspeed Oxford and de Havilland Tiger Moth trainers. Uneasiness about the idea of a totally unarmed bomber had also developed, but interest in a long-range fighter version had begun and so the original programme

was changed to 20 bombers and 30 fighters; it was unsettled whether the latter should be single- or dual-control or should carry a turret, so three prototypes were required. This caused delays while half-completed spars and wings had to be strengthened for the anticipated higher fighter combat load requirements, and bomber-type fuselage noses with clear nose cones already completed had to be altered for the new 'solid-nose' fighter version.

During the autumn of 1940 the work of building the initial Mosquito prototype went ahead, despite a serious German air raid on 3 October that caused considerable damage at Hatfield. The Mosquito prototype was constructed in a small hanger erected at Salisbury Hall and disguised as a barn. On 3 November the aircraft was transported by road to Hatfield where it was put into a small blast-proof building for reassembly, and successful engine runs were made on 19 November. On 25 November 1940 it made its first flight, piloted by Geoffrey de Havilland, Jr. This initial flight was performed four days short of 11 months from the start of detail design work, a remarkable achievement particularly under the conditions of the time. The prototype was painted bright yellow, it has been claimed to give the often

Resplendent in its overall yellow colouring, the prototype D.H. 98 serialled E0234 (later W4050) is seen at Hatfield, showing the clean lines of the design and confirming its light colouring. Note the short engine nacelles (Photo: HSA).

trigger-happy British anti-aircraft gunners a chance of recognising its unfamiliar shape. It made two flights in 'B' Condition markings as E0234, thereafter gaining the military serial number W4050.

From the start it was clear the new aircraft was a winner. Its performance was impressive, being fast and highly manoeuvrable. Company trials of W4050 were completed during the three worst winter months, and established the Mosquito as arguably the world's fastest combat aircraft (although it was not encumbered with a full military load under operational conditions at that time) – it was definitely streets ahead of the light bombers such as the Bristol Blenheim then in RAF service. Modifications as a result of the initial company trials were few, the most troublesome being the extension of the engine nacelles aft of the wing trailing edges which involved dividing the wing flaps. On 19 February 1941 W4050 was handed over to the RAF for official trials at the A&AEE Boscombe Down. These trials were almost without trouble, again proving the success of the design, but a structural failure in the rear fuselage was detected. Meanwhile, de Havilland had been instructed to convert the 20 initial bomber Mosquitoes for photographic reconnaissance, but later they were instructed to finish ten of them as bombers, these becoming the first true Mosquito bombers as B.Mk. IV series I machines.

Construction Details

The Mosquito's oval-section fuselage was built in two halves in jigs over a mahogany or concrete basic shape, the join between the two halves being along the vertical centre line. Seven bulkheads made up of two plywood skins separated by spruce blocks formed the basis on each half for the outer shell, which was a sandwich of balsa wood between two layers of plywood. Glue, including strong Casein glue, plus many screws and wooden flanges, held the whole structure together. After mating together of the two halves the whole fuselage structure was covered with fabric, which was then doped with red cellulose dope (either brushed on or sprayed). A coat of silver dope was finally applied before the application of the exterior coats of outer camouflage paint. The underside of the fuselage shell was subsequently precision cut out to allow the wing to be attached. The wing attachment was by means of four large and strong attachment points. The lower portion of the cut-out, suitably cut back itself, was then replaced after the wing had been attached.

The all-wood wing was built as a one-piece structure. It was made up of two box spars, spruce and plywood compression ribs, spruce stringers, and a plywood covering. The outer plywood skin was covered with fabric and doped like the fuselage. Low-drag radiators for the liquid-cooling of the two Merlin engines were fitted just outboard of the fuselage in the wing leading edges. For the fighter versions of the Mosquito, which were expected to require a higher g-loading, the wing structure was suitably strengthened at key points with stronger or additional structural members. The ailerons were metal framed and skinned, but the hydraulically-operated wing flaps were all-wood. The engine nacelles were predominantly wood, but fixings and mounts for the engines were metal, as of course was the undercarriage. The hydraulically-activated undercarriage itself contained a stack of rubber blocks within the main struts for shock-absorbing, a somewhat unusual method for that particular period. The tail unit of the Mosquito was of all-wood construction, but the moveable surfaces (elevators and rudder) were metal (aluminium) framed and fabric-covered.

Successful Test Flying

The Mosquito stimulated much interest from the start during its test flying, and any official doubts about the project were quickly put to rest. With a level speed clean of just over 400 mph (644 km/h), excellent single-engine performance including the ability to climb with one engine feathered (unthinkable for many twin-engined front-line types at that time), the Mosquito was set for an outstanding service career. The next prototype of the three that were actually built was W4052, which in effect was the F.Mk.II fighter prototype and related to official Specification F.21/40. It made its first flight on 15 May 1941, and subsequently pioneered the Mosquito as a night-fighter, being fitted with AI (Airborne Interception) Mk.IV radar, a flat bullet-proof windscreen as opposed to the pointed windscreen of W4050 and subsequent bomber versions, and a new armament fit. The latter comprised four 0.303 in (7.7 mm) Browning machine

W4051 was one of three main prototypes for the D.H. 98 line. It was the development aircraft for the planned reconnaissance production versions of the Mosquito. The location of the photograph is believed to be Benson, which was the home of the RAF's aerial photography efforts during World War Two. Early Mosquitoes were powered by the 1,280 hp single-stage, two-speed supercharged Merlin 21 engine. Later the slightly more powerful Merlin 23 was introduced into Mosquito production, with the 1,620 hp Merlin 25 engine subsequently powering major early marks like the later FB.Mk.VI production Mosquitoes (Photo: M.V. Lowe Collection).

guns in the extreme nose, and four 20 mm Hispano cannons in the lower forward fuselage beneath the cockpit. At one stage an early Mosquito was temporarily fitted with a dummy Bristol gun turret behind the cockpit, but no production Mosquitoes were so equipped.

The final Mosquito prototype to fly was W4051, which first flew on 10 June 1941. This was the precursor of the initial PR.Mk.I reconnaissance model, and pioneered the use of the Mosquito as an unarmed fast camera-carrying reconnaissance aircraft. After a short spell at Boscombe Down on official trials, it was moved in July to Benson in Oxfordshire, the home of the RAF's reconnaissance efforts in World War Two. Completed production Mosquitoes started to appear in July 1941, and in the same month production orders for substantial numbers of Mosquitoes began to amass. Commencing on 7 August, the first production Mosquito PR.I aircraft (from the first production batch, W4054-W4063) were delivered to the RAF, and the Mosquito started to enter combat as soon as possible. No.1 P.R.U. (Photographic Reconnaissance Unit) was the initial recipient, and this unit flew the first Mosquito operational sortie on 17 September 1941.

Above right:
The Author's Father, Victor Lowe, with a Mosquito coded TW-F of No.141 Squadron in the late 1940's. The prominent strengthening strip on the fuselage side is clearly visible (Photo: Victor Lowe).

Right:
The fuselage side of a Mosquito under construction. The inner three-ply birch skin lies neatly contoured to the mahogany mould shape, with structural strengthening members attached to it. Between these structural members, balsa wood will later be added to fill up the inner portion of the sandwich, with the whole then covered with the outer skin of three-ply birch plywood. This fuselage half is for a bomber Mosquito with a clear nose, because the forward fuselage ends in a diagonal curve and part of the rectangular shape for the nose side window can just be seen at the extreme right-hand end of the inner skin (Photo: British Aerospace).

A very early production Mosquito night-fighter, NF.Mk.II DD609, shows off its overall Night (black) or possibly matt RDM 2A colouring and Dull Red serial number, and its full equipment fit. With AI Mk.IV radar installed, the prominent 'arrow head' nose fitting and wing aerials are visible. (Photo: HSA).

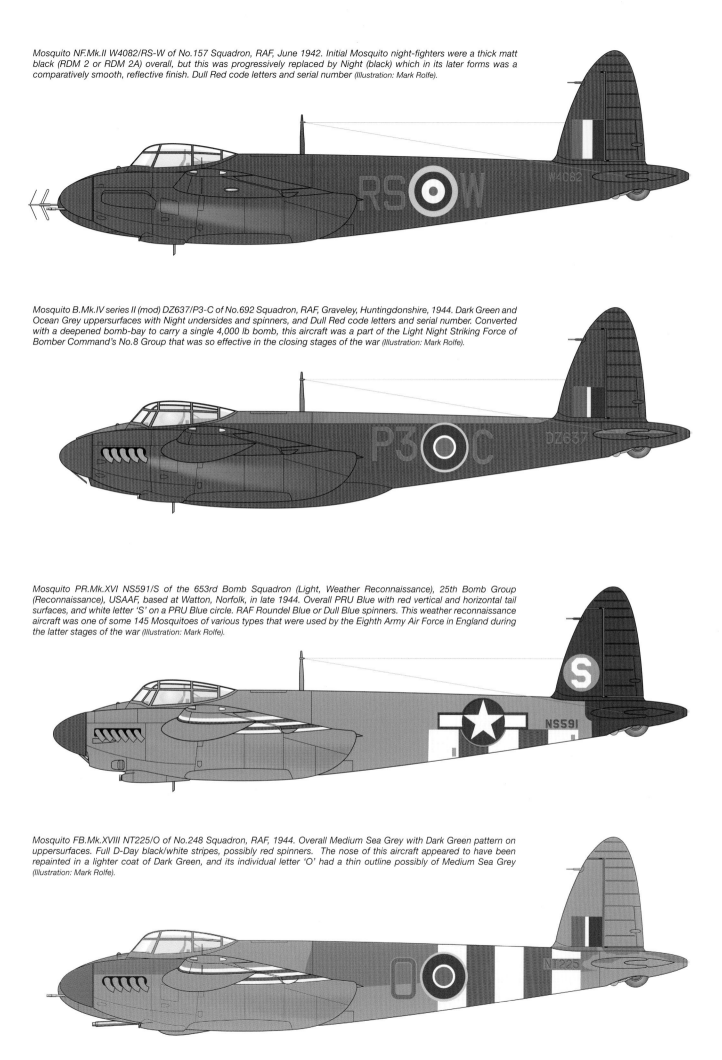

Mosquito NF.Mk.II W4082/RS-W of No.157 Squadron, RAF, June 1942. Initial Mosquito night-fighters were a thick matt black (RDM 2 or RDM 2A) overall, but this was progressively replaced by Night (black) which in its later forms was a comparatively smooth, reflective finish. Dull Red code letters and serial number (Illustration: Mark Rolfe).

Mosquito B.Mk.IV series II (mod) DZ637/P3-C of No.692 Squadron, RAF, Graveley, Huntingdonshire, 1944. Dark Green and Ocean Grey uppersurfaces with Night undersides and spinners, and Dull Red code letters and serial number. Converted with a deepened bomb-bay to carry a single 4,000 lb bomb, this aircraft was a part of the Light Night Striking Force of Bomber Command's No.8 Group that was so effective in the closing stages of the war (Illustration: Mark Rolfe).

Mosquito PR.Mk.XVI NS591/S of the 653rd Bomb Squadron (Light, Weather Reconnaissance), 25th Bomb Group (Reconnaissance), USAAF, based at Watton, Norfolk, in late 1944. Overall PRU Blue with red vertical and horizontal tail surfaces, and white letter 'S' on a PRU Blue circle. RAF Roundel Blue or Dull Blue spinners. This weather reconnaissance aircraft was one of some 145 Mosquitoes of various types that were used by the Eighth Army Air Force in England during the latter stages of the war (Illustration: Mark Rolfe).

Mosquito FB.Mk.XVIII NT225/O of No.248 Squadron, RAF, 1944. Overall Medium Sea Grey with Dark Green pattern on uppersurfaces. Full D-Day black/white stripes, possibly red spinners. The nose of this aircraft appeared to have been repainted in a lighter coat of Dark Green, and its individual letter 'O' had a thin outline possibly of Medium Sea Grey (Illustration: Mark Rolfe).

From early in the development life of the Mosquito, manufacture was planned and then carried out in a variety of locations, including outside Britain. This is one of the first Canadian-built Mosquitoes in late 1943 to reach Britain, a B.Mk.XX named for Moose Jaw, Saskatchewan (Photo: HSA).

Chapter 2 Wartime Service

Initial operations by the first reconnaissance Mosquitoes proved the quality of the Mosquito layout, and also showed the type's excellent range - with sorties being flown all over Occupied Europe including France, Central Europe and northern Norway from bases in Britain. Although the photo-reconnaissance Mosquito was the first to enter service, both the early production bomber and fighter variants of the Mosquito were soon being produced in numbers. Initial bomber Mosquitoes were of the B.Mk. IV layout, the first being the batch of approximately 10 early B.IV series I (although not all were apparently finished to that standard), followed by the first Mosquito bomber version, the B.IV series II. This had the long engine nacelles extending behind the wing trailing edge that were characteristic of subsequent Mosquito production models, and other important refinements including the ability to carry four 500 lb (227 kg) bombs with abbreviated fins within the fuselage bomb-bay, giving the otherwise unarmed Mk.IV a considerable punch.

The first squadron to operate the B.Mk.IV was the RAF's No.105 Squadron at Swanton Morley, Norfolk, which received its first B.IV (an early series I aircraft, W4064) in November 1941 – although the unit's first major operation was on 31 May 1942, a daylight attack on Cologne as a follow-up to the '1,000 bomber raid' on this city in the previous night. Showing the fine range capabilities of the Mosquito, on 19 September 1942 six aircraft of the squadron attempted the first daylight raid of the type on Berlin. The Mosquito was obviously a significant addition to the RAF's growing bomber capabilities, and the first of a string of pinpoint specialist raids was carried out on 25 September when Mosquitoes of No.105 Squadron bombed the Gestapo headquarters in Oslo. Thereafter several more squadrons converted onto the type, and the range of weapons available to the Mosquito expanded – this included the development of a deepened bomb-bay for some 26 of the B.IV version

Mosquito NF.Mk.II DD750, devoid of AI aerials, these either having been removed for security reasons if the aircraft was likely to fly over enemy-held territory, or simply painted out by the wartime censor. The original matt Night (black) colouring was replaced on some aircraft by a smoother black with a slight sheen (Photo: HSA).

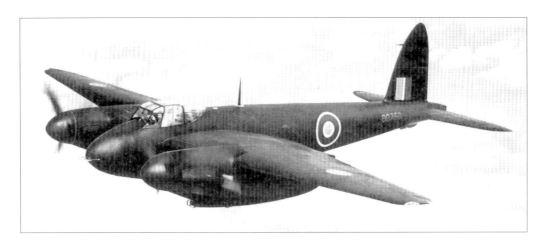

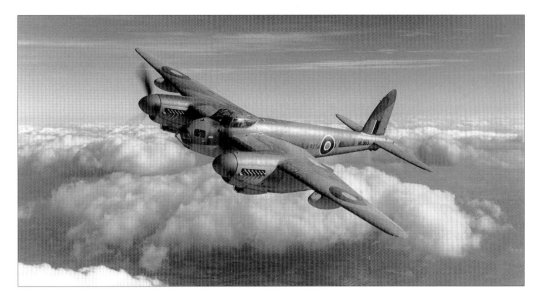

to house a 4,000 lb (1,814 kg) bomb (pioneered with trials involving B.IV series II DZ594), thus giving the Mosquito almost the bomb load of a heavy bomber. No.692 Squadron first used this combination on 23/24 February 1944 against targets in Düsseldorf. Both Nos.105 and 139 Squadrons became a part of the Pathfinder Force of Bomber Command's No.8 Group in the summer of 1943, flying their Mosquitoes ahead of heavy bomber attacks and employing the navigation aid 'Oboe' to precision mark targets for the main bomber force. Some Mosquitoes were also configured for the use of the 'Highball' spherical bomb, pioneered in trials with DK290, which would have been used by Mosquitoes against Japanese shipping in the Far East if the Second World War had

continued into 1946.

It is as a fighter and fighter-bomber that the Mosquito is most often remembered, however. With its crew of two and capability to carry the relevant on-board radar equipment, the Mosquito was viewed by de Havilland as a natural choice for adaptation into the then developing art of night fighting. After successful trials with prototype W4052, the initial production night-fighter variant of the Mosquito was the NF.Mk.II. The RAF's No.157 Squadron was the first to receive the type in late 1941/early 1942, obtaining its initial aircraft (W4073, one of several early Mosquitoes that had the possibility for dual controls and approximated to a T.Mk.III trainer) on 26 January 1942 at Castle Camps in East Anglia. This squadron

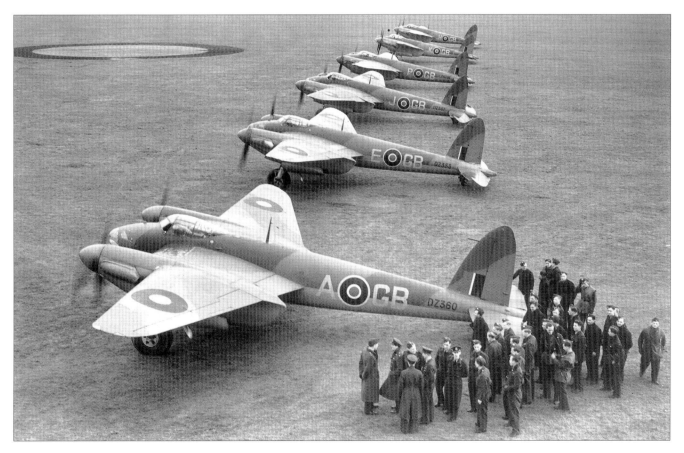

became operational later in the year, by which time No.23 Squadron at Ford in Hampshire had also converted onto the NF.II. The first confirmed Mosquito aerial victory, a Dornier Do 217, was achieved by the latter squadron on 6/7 July 1942 over Montdidier in France. No.23 Squadron subsequently moved to Malta in December 1942 where it flew its Mosquitoes on night interception and intruder missions, over the island of Malta itself and over Sicily and Italy. Night-fighter radar developments followed swiftly during the war. The initial AI Mk.IV radar of the early NF.II Mosquitoes with its distinctive 'arrow head' antennae protruding from the nose was superseded by the introduction of centimetric radar using a rotating dish installed in the extreme forward fuselage, initially of the AI Mk.VIII variety. The first Mosquito version to use this new radar, which involved the deletion of the four 0.303 in (7.7 mm) Browning machine guns in the extreme nose, was the NF.Mk.XII – 97 of the planned 466 production NF.II Mosquitoes were finished to this standard, and paved the way for further night fighter models that are described in the following chapter. There were a number of important alterations between the bomber and night-fighter Mosquito variants, in addition to the different crew layout in the cockpit to allow the second crew member to operate the night-fighter radar alongside the pilot. These included the introduction of a flat windscreen that became standard for subsequent fighter and fighter-bomber Mosquitoes rather than the pointed windscreen layout of the pure bomber Mosquitoes, and a different means of crew access, in which the

night-fighter crew boarded the aircraft through a side door rather than the lower fuselage access of the bomber Mosquitoes. Night-fighter Mosquitoes in several marks provided sterling service in the night-time aerial defence of Britain later in the war. Mosquitoes also claimed an impressive tally, from mid-1944, of some 623 V1 flying bombs.

The growth potential of the Mosquito was revealed again in the adaptation of the type into the day-time fighter-bomber role, effectively combining the separate fighter and bomber configurations of the early production Mosquitoes. This resulted in the FB.Mk.VI (first flight 1 June 1942, first production delivery February 1943), which had a combined machine gun and bomb armament, able to carry up to 2,000 lb (907 kg) of bombs in its rear weapons bay and on underwing attachments but retaining the four cannons and four machine gun armament of the initial fighter/night-fighter Mosquitoes. This version could also be fitted with more powerful Merlin 25 engines of 1,620 hp each for take-off, and was later configured to carry up to four unguided rockets beneath each wing. In that layout the type proved lethal for anti-shipping operations, and a number were used by RAF Coastal Command squadrons specifically for this demanding and particularly dangerous role, most famously by units of the Banff Strike Wing in Scotland which primarily operated over the waters off the Norwegian coast and northern Atlantic.

The fighter-bomber Mosquito variants combined the hard-hitting forward-firing cannon and machine gun armament of the fighter Mosquitoes with a bomb-bay behind the cannon mountings in the lower fuselage, and a flat windscreen. Entry into the fighter and fighter-bomber Mosquitoes was via an entrance door in the right-hand fuselage side ahead of the wing, accessed with an extendable boarding ladder as shown here (Photo: Library of Congress).

Sea Mosquito TR.Mk.33 TW281, showing the type's lower rear fuselage arrestor hook, four-bladed propellers, and completely revised main undercarriage legs (Photo: HSA).

Chapter 3 Mosquito Versions and Roles

The Mosquito played a very extensive part in the air war particularly over Europe following its combat introduction in the bomber role during May 1942, and in a variety of versions it was an important factor in the RAF's contribution to victory in 1945. Despite early misgivings about its mainly wood construction, the Mosquito proved to be rugged and able to take a considerable amount of punishment. Development lines included fighters and fighter-bombers, bombers, reconnaissance aircraft, navalised examples and trainers, but in practice Mosquitoes performed virtually every role expected of combat aircraft during the Second World War. The term 'Wooden Wonder' has often, rightly, been used to describe this outstanding aircraft. The equally excellent Rolls-Royce Merlin inline liquid-cooled piston engine powered the Mosquito; many of these were British-built, but some (including the 225, 31 and 33, and 69 versions), were built in the US by Packard, the American wartime licence-producer of Merlin engines.

Bombers

In addition to the highly-successful B.Mk.IV variant referred to in the previous Chapter, several further bomber versions of the Mosquito were built. The Mosquito bombers proved highly successful and adaptable, operating firstly by day, and then primarily at night from mid-1943 when flown as a part of the Pathfinder Force previously noted. Mosquito bombers also operated as a part of a Bomber Command organisation known as the Light Night Striking Force, which attacked specific industrial and other high-value targets at night, utilising the Mosquito's

exceptional range and load-carrying abilities. Flown by some of the most capable and gifted aircrews in Bomber Command, the Mosquito bomber force was a significant if often unsung part of the wartime British bombing effort against Germany. In addition to the B.Mk.IV, there were the following bomber versions -

B.Mk.V: Prototype, not itself built in series, and was a development of the B.Mk.IV with underwing hardpoints to carry two 50 Imperial gallon (227 litre) streamlined underwing fuel tanks, or two 500 lb (227 kg) bombs. It was the basis for the Canadian-built B.Mk.VII referred to later.

B.Mk.IX: High-altitude version of the B.Mk.IV, powered by two 1,280 hp Rolls-Royce Merlin 72 engines with two-speed, two-stage superchargers. The 'Standard Wing', introduced on the B.Mk.V prototype, was fitted allowing a maximum bomb load of 3,000 lb (1,361 kg) with the addition of underwing bombs. If required, however, the bomb-bay and underwing hardpoints could be used to carry additional fuel. Some were converted to carry one 4,000 lb (1,814 kg) 'block-buster' or 'cookie' bomb, with the provision of the enlarged 'bulged' bomb-bay.

B.Mk.XVI: A development of the B.Mk.IX, with Merlin 72 or 76 (right-hand) and Merlin 73 or 77 (left-hand) engines, the latter powering a supercharger for cockpit pressurization. Most if not all were completed to accommodate a 4,000 lb (1,814 kg) 'block-buster' or 'cookie' bomb internally, and could also carry two wing-mounted 50 Imperial gallon (227 litre) fuel tanks or four 500 lb (227 kg) bombs internally plus two 100 Imperial gallon (454 litre) drop tanks, with which a

Mosquito B.Mk.IX LR500 with Merlin 72 engines of 1,280 hp each. This was one of the first significant marks of Mosquito in which the more capable 60-series two-stage, two-speed supercharged Merlin engine was installed regularly, and so represented the second major phase of Mosquito power plant development compared to the single-stage supercharged Merlin XX-series engines of the earlier Mosquitoes. These later, two-stage Merlin-equipped Mosquitoes had slightly longer engine installations, and were readily identified by the prominent 'chin' intercooler radiator air intake beneath each forward engine cowling (Photo: HSA).

range of 1,470 miles (2,366 km) was possible. This was one of the main Mosquito bombers.

B.Mk.35: Developed from the B.Mk.XVI, with Merlin 113/114 engines. This was the final British-built bomber Mosquito variant, the last example in de Havilland manufacture was at Hatfield (TK656) in April 1946. The type served principally with Nos.109 and 139 Squadrons post-war, and was replaced by English Electric Canberra jet bombers in 1952-3. There were important post-war conversions to TT.35 target-towers, plus a small number of PR.35.

Trainers and Transports

T.Mk.III: An unarmed dual-control version, based roughly on the F.II layout, used mainly but not exclusively for conversion to the front-line Mosquitoes, powered by the Merlin 21, 23 or 25 engines. This was the principal trainer derivative of the Mosquito, some 343 being constructed. The Canadian-built T.Mk.22 and later marks, and the Australian T.Mk.43 (the latter being the highest-numbered Mosquito variant) were similar.

Mk.IV/VI: Ten Mosquitoes were employed as fast transports, bearing civil registrations and operated by British Overseas Airways Corporation (BOAC). Based on the FB.Mk.VI (although the first was a converted B.IV) but with a modified interior for carrying a passenger or limited but high-value cargo in the converted bomb-bay, these aircraft were used for a variety of tasks, notably but not exclusively flying between Britain and neutral Sweden carrying VIPs, escaped prisoners of war, and ball bearings.

Fighters and Fighter-Bombers

The Mosquito is well-known for its role as a night-fighter, and this task was a vital component of the British defences from 1942 onwards. By mid-1943 12 night-fighter squadrons were operating Mosquitoes, and the type was a significant part of the Air Defence of Great Britain organisation (the temporary and much disliked re-naming of RAF's Fighter Command) during 1944. Mosquito night-fighters also flew as a part of Bomber Command's No.100 Group to provide protection for the RAF's heavy bombers against

Mosquito NF.Mk.36 night-fighter RL240 (Photo: HSA).

German night-fighters on their nighttime operations over Occupied Europe. These nocturnal missions over Europe eventually led to the Mosquitoes carrying bombs on occasion for attacks on suitable enemy targets, although by the end of the war the formidable, jet-powered Messerschmitt Me 262 started to appear over Germany and proved to be a match for the Mosquito's previous speed advantage. One of the celebrated British pilots of the Second World War, John "Cat's Eyes" Cunningham, was a Mosquito night-fighter pilot – although night-fighting was very much a team effort between the pilot and radar-operator aboard the aircraft, and ground radar stations. In the related line of development, Mosquito fighter-bombers combined the best elements of the fighter and bomber Mosquitoes for armed daylight attacks on enemy ground targets, although long-

Hatfield during February 1943. Provision was made in 1944 to carry four unguided rocket projectiles on pylons below each wing. Built by de Havilland, Airspeed, and Standard Motors, with some 2,300 built as the most numerous of Mosquito variants.

FB.Mk.XVIII: Development of the FB.Mk.VI. with Merlin 25 engines, some 27 were completed with a Molins 57 mm (six-pounder) converted anti-tank gun in the lower nose/fuselage instead of the 20 mm cannons, for anti-submarine and anti-shipping work with the RAF's Coastal Command. Armour protection was provided for the crew and engines.

NF.Mk.XII: A conversion of 97 NF.Mk.IIs, with Merlin 21, 23 or 25 engines, four lower fuselage 20 mm cannon, and the new AI Mk.VIII centimetric radar. The four nose-mounted 0.303 in (7.7 mm) machine guns were deleted.

Mosquito FB.Mk.XVIII PZ468 QM-D of No.254 Squadron, RAF, at North Coates, Lincolnshire, was one of the rare Molins gun-equipped Mosquitoes. The end of the barrel of the large-calibre Molins gun can be seen protruding under the forward fuselage in the detail picture at left. Usually just two of the four nose machine guns were fitted on this mark (Photos: HSA).

range night intruder missions were also very much a Mosquito speciality, both over Europe and against the Japanese in the Far East. The main production models were as follows -

FB.Mk.VI: Developed from the Mk.II fighter prototype, with fighter armament, and powered by Merlin 21, 23 or 1,620 hp Merlin 25 engines. Fitted with the 'Standard Wing', it could carry up to 2,000 lb (907 kg) of bombs in its abbreviated fuselage bomb-bay and under the wings. The first was completed at

NF.Mk.XIII: New-production counterpart of NF.Mk. XII, with increased wing fuel due to having a wing layout similar to the FB.VI for underwing drop tanks or bombs.

NF.Mk.XV: Special small quantity high-altitude night-fighter version to combat Junkers Ju 86P high-flying reconnaissance aircraft, based on B.Mk. IV bombers but with two-stage Merlins. Extended wingtips, AI Mk.VIII radar, and a specially-designed underfuselage armament arrangement of four 0.303

Hatfield-built Mosquito PR.Mk. XVI NS624. Note the oblique camera window below and ahead of the red and blue fuselage roundel on this dedicated reconnaissance aircraft. The overall colour of many of the PR Mosquitoes was PRU Blue (Photo: HSA).

de Havilland Mosquito FB.Mk.VI series II

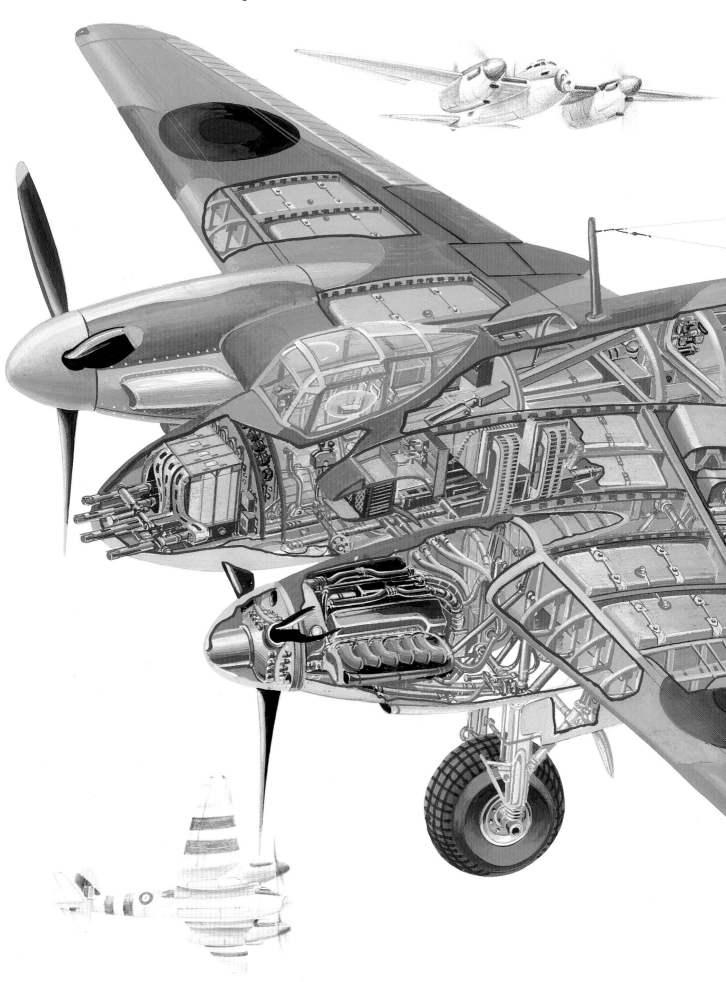

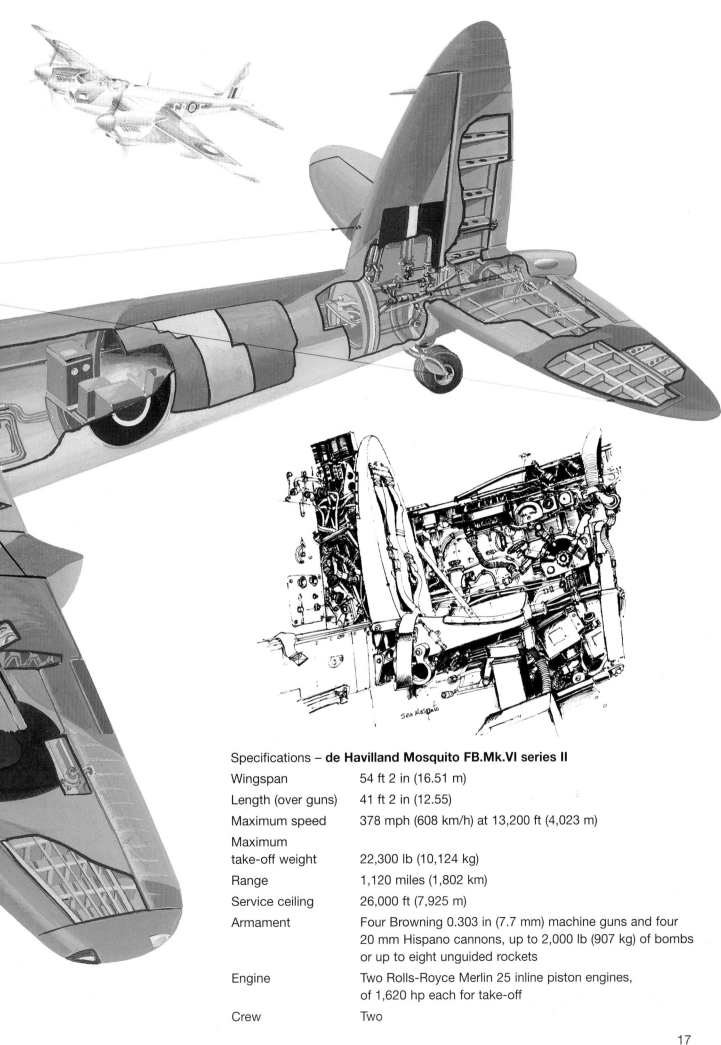

sea Mosquito

Specifications – **de Havilland Mosquito FB.Mk.VI series II**

Wingspan	54 ft 2 in (16.51 m)
Length (over guns)	41 ft 2 in (12.55)
Maximum speed	378 mph (608 km/h) at 13,200 ft (4,023 m)
Maximum take-off weight	22,300 lb (10,124 kg)
Range	1,120 miles (1,802 km)
Service ceiling	26,000 ft (7,925 m)
Armament	Four Browning 0.303 in (7.7 mm) machine guns and four 20 mm Hispano cannons, up to 2,000 lb (907 kg) of bombs or up to eight unguided rockets
Engine	Two Rolls-Royce Merlin 25 inline piston engines, of 1,620 hp each for take-off
Crew	Two

in (7.7 mm) machine guns.

NF.Mk.XVII: Developed from the NF.Mk.XIII, and equipped with AI Mk.X or American SCR-720 radar.

NF.Mk.XIX: Developed from the NF.Mk.XIII with Merlin 25 engines, increased maximum take-off weight, and able to carry AI Mk.VIII, AI Mk.X, or SCR-720 radar.

NF.Mk.30: High-altitude development of the NF.Mk.XIX, with 1,280 hp Merlin 72 or 1,250 hp Merlin 76 engines, AI Mk.X radar, and early ECM (electronic counter-measures)-type equipment. Maximum speed was an excellent 424 mph (682 km/h).

NF.Mk.36: Post-war development of the NF.Mk.30, with 1,710 hp Merlin 113 engines.

NF.Mk.38: The final British-built fighter version, which was a development of the NF.36 with AI Mk.IX radar.

Reconnaissance

Photographic reconnaissance Mosquitoes were built in a variety of versions, and this role became a very important task for the Mosquito family. Following the initial operational reconnaissance Mosquitoes of August and September 1941, the Mosquito gradually took over long-range reconnaissance missions from reconnaissance-configured Spitfires, and successfully continued in this role until the end of the war and beyond. The first reconnaissance Mosquitoes were to PR.I standard, and were followed by these marks -

PR.Mk.IV: At least 29 converted from B.Mk.IVs, with provision for up to four cameras in place of bomb load.

PR.Mk.VIII: Five examples, generally similar to the B.Mk.IV, but powered by 1,280 hp special Merlin 61 supercharged engines for high-altitude work as a stop-gap until the PR.IX was ready.

PR.Mk.IX: Photographic reconnaissance variant of B.Mk.IX, first flight in April 1943, with provision for extra long-range capability with two 200 Imperial gallon (909 litre) fuel drop tanks.

PR.Mk.XVI: Photographic reconnaissance variant of B.Mk.XVI, as the first pressurised PR version; introduced small astrodome on starboard upper surface of cockpit canopy (just over 430 built) and first flew in the summer of 1943.

PR.Mk.32: Five converted from PR.Mk.XVIs with extended wingtips (span 59 ft 2 in – 18 m) and Merlin 113 engines (right-hand) and 114 (left-hand), employed on high-altitude reconnaissance work.

PR.Mk.34: Very long-range reconnaissance version intended specifically for use in South-East Asia, with two 200 Imperial gallon (909 litre) drop tanks which, together with additional fuel tankage in its 'bulged' lower fuselage had a range of up to 3,500 miles (5,633 km). Merlin 76 or 113 engines. This became the main photographic reconnaissance type to serve in the RAF immediately after the war.

Sea Mosquitoes

In a separate but related line of development, the Mosquito was navalised to suit specific requirements for Britain's Royal Navy. Initial attempts were made to test the suitability of the Mosquito for aircraft carrier operation in 1944. The well-known naval pilot Capt (at that time Lt, later Lt Cdr) Eric Brown made the first deck landing, aboard HMS *Indefatigable* in a modified FB.VI (LR359), on 25 March 1944. The tests proved the feasibility of the concept, but Mosquitoes were later used by the Royal Navy's Fleet Air Arm for second-line and Fleet Requirements duties, and not front-line roles. The Royal Navy also operated former RAF Mosquitoes, principally the FB.VI, PR.XVI, and T.III. Specific naval versions were as follows –

TF.(later TR.)33: torpedo/reconnaissance fighter or fighter-bomber for aircraft carrier operation, based on the FB.VI. Merlin 25 engines, four-bladed propellers, oleo-pneumatic main undercarriage legs rather than the rubber blocks shock-absorbing method, folding outer wings, arrestor hook. Provision for rocket-assisted take-off (RATO) equipment. American ASH nose radar. Four 20 mm cannons. Internal bomb load or 2,000 lb (907 kg) torpedo or mine, plus underwing stores similar to FB.VI. 50 completed, some served until 1953.

TF/TR.37: derivative of the TR.33, with British ASV Mk.XIII radar.

TT.39: target-towing derivative of the B.Mk.XVI by General Aircraft Ltd, comprising a new extended and glazed forward fuselage for a camera operator, and a dorsal observation cupola, at least some with Merlin 72/73 engines. Fuselage length increased to 43 ft 4 in (13.21 m). Some 35 were converted from Mk.XVI production, examples serving until the early 1950's.

The Royal Navy flew a number of specific navalised Mosquito versions, including the TR.Mk.37, of which TW240 seen here (a former TR.33) acted as a development prototype. The lower rear fuselage arrestor hook, four-bladed propellers, and completely revised main undercarriage legs of Fleet Air Arm Mosquitoes can be seen in this view. Naval Mosquitoes had manually-folding wings (Photo: HSA).

Foreign Production

In addition to production in Britain, Mosquitoes were also manufactured in Canada and Australia. Planning for overseas production at de Havilland subsidiaries in these two countries began in earnest in the summer of 1941, and in the event both countries contributed significantly to overall Mosquito production. Australian-built Mosquitoes served primarily in the Far East, but some of the

The final Mosquito version for the Royal Navy was the TT.39, as exemplified here by PF606, a former B.XVI that was converted by General Aircraft Ltd. Identified serial numbers of Mosquitoes that were re-modelled into TT.39 target-towing standard suggest that 35 examples were so converted (Photo: M.V. Lowe Collection).

Canadian production was destined specifically for Britain and used by the RAF. Details of the variants built in Canada and Australia are as follows:

Canada:

B.Mk.VII: Canadian-built version of the B.Mk.V prototype, powered by two 1,300 hp Packard Merlin 31 engines (25 built – six of these were converted for reconnaissance duties with the USAAF under the designation F-8).

B.Mk.XX: Similar to the B.Mk.VII, but with US or Canadian equipment. 245 were built, 34 became F-8 for the USAAF.

B.Mk.25: Successor to the B.Mk.XX, powered by 1,635 hp Packard Merlin 225 engines.

FB.Mk.21: Similar to the British-built FB.Mk.VI, but with Packard Merlin 31/33 engines (3 built).

FB.Mk.26: Development of the British FB.Mk.VI, powered by Packard Merlin 225 engines.

T.Mk.22: Dual-control trainer built in small numbers, related to the British T.III, with Merlin 33 engines, similar to FB.Mk.21.

T.Mk.27: Dual-control trainer development of the T.Mk.22, with Packard Merlin 225 engines.

T.Mk.29: Dual-control trainer based on the FB.Mk.26 with Packard Merlin 225 engines.

Australia:

FB.Mk.40: First Australian-built version, generally similar to British FB.Mk.VI, powered by 1,300 hp Packard Merlin 31 or 33 engines. The first example

flew in July 1943 (212 built, some as other marks). Six converted to PR.40.

PR.Mk.41: Dedicated reconnaissance version related to the PR.Mk.IX and FB.40, with Packard Merlin 69 engines.

T.Mk.43: Two-seat dual-control trainer version of the FB.40, with Packard Merlin 33 engines, generally similar to the British T.III trainer.

Although Mosquito variants were numbered up to the Mk.43, several designations (for example the Mk.XI) were not used, but some were duplicated (for example the B.IV and PR.IV, and the FB.VI fighter-bomber and Mk.VI transport). The exact number of Mosquitoes that were actually completed has long been a source of dispute amongst historians. The total of 7,781 is usually accepted as being a good approximation, but 7,619 is also regularly quoted. Mosquitoes were built in Britain by de Havilland at Hatfield, Leavesden, and Chester, and by Standard Motors, Percival, and Airspeed; production in Canada was by de Havilland at Downsview, Ontario; and by de Havilland in Australia at Mascot, Sydney, New South Wales. The final Mosquito to be built was an NF.Mk.38, constructed at de Havilland's Chester factory in Britain and delivered on 28 November 1950.

KA117 was a Canadian-built Mosquito T.Mk.29 (Photo: HSA).

A detail view of the unusual and ungainly nose contours of the Royal Navy's TT.39, shown off here in solid mock-up form by one of the TT.39 prototypes, PF489 (Photo: M. V. Lowe Collection).

Several Mosquitoes were employed for trials work. B.Mk.XVI ML926/G was converted for H2S bombing radar experimental testing, and flew at Boscombe Down in May and June 1944 for development work on 'Oboe' bombing aid repeater gear, the relevant equipment being mounted in the large non-standard fairing visible below the aircraft's fuselage (Photo: M.V. Lowe Collection).

Chapter 4 Trials and Post-war Service

The end of World War Two was by no means the end of the Mosquito's service, and the type continued to operate with the RAF and with Commonwealth air forces for some time to come. Mosquitoes were also exported widely to overseas customers, as explained in the next Chapter.

The Mosquito continued to give valuable service to the RAF in the years following the Second World War. Amongst the tasks delegated to front-line Mosquito units was to be a part of the post-war British occupation forces in Germany. Reconnaissance Mosquitoes performed important service around the world, including operations in the Middle and Far East where survey and mapping work was carried out, in addition to service during the campaign against communist forces in Malaya (Operation *Firedog*), and in the troubled mandate of Palestine during the creation of the state of Israel. No.81 Squadron in Malaya was the last unit to use the Mosquito operationally, with that squadron's PR.Mk.34 RG314 making the final operational sortie of a Mosquito in RAF service on 15 December 1955. By then the remaining bomber Mosquitoes had been replaced by English Electric Canberra turbojet-powered bombers in 1952-3, although various examples were then employed in the training role, with some converted for target-towing – a significant number of the B.Mk.35 variant were

converted into TT.35 standard to tow targets. Some of the latter remained in service until 1963, the final unit to fly them being No.3 Civilian Anti-Aircraft Co-operation Unit (CAACU) at Exeter in Devon.

Many former military Mosquitoes made their way to civilian owners after the Second World War, for a wide variety of tasks. Some were employed for air racing in the US, whilst in Canada several were used for survey work by Spartan Air Services. One, a Canadian-built B.25 civil registered in the US as N1203V, was used in a failed attempt to break the round-the-world speed record. However, the best-known civil Mosquitoes – including several which survived in CAACU service in Britain – were those employed in film work, notably in the Mirisch Films motion picture '633 Squadron'. Thanks to this film work several of these Mosquitoes survive to the present day.

Mosquito TT.Mk.35 target-tower, RS719, shows off its silver finish with yellow fuselage and wing bands. The aircraft was converted from a B.Mk.35, and wore black and 'Trainer Yellow' undersides. Note the target-towing winch below the fuselage and towing cable guards on the tailplane (Photo: HSA).

Chapter 5 Foreign Service

A large number of Mosquitoes, possibly as many as one thousand, served with foreign operators in addition to British service. Much of this overseas use was after World War Two, and in some cases it is impossible to verify the exact numbers involved due to the confused or clandestine nature of some of these deliveries and subsequent service. Mosquitoes were in effect not built specifically for foreign operators as export models outside the deliveries for British or Commonwealth countries, and many that were sold overseas after the war were former RAF machines that were refurbished prior to their further use, by companies such as Airspeed at Portsmouth in Hampshire, or Fairey Aviation at Ringway, Manchester.

Several Commonwealth countries, including South Africa, New Zealand, possibly Burma, Canada, and Australia, operated Mosquitoes in addition to the latter two actually building the type. In South African Air Force service reconnaissance Mosquitoes flew during World War Two, with No.60 Squadron from early 1943 in North Africa and southern Europe. The squadron later standardized mainly on the PR.XVI, and returned to South Africa with approximately ten of its Mosquitoes after the end of the war in Europe. A small number of F.II Mosquito fighters were also flown by South African crews. New Zealand ordered 80 FB.VI from British stocks for the Royal New Zealand Air Force (76 were eventually delivered), and also obtained four T.43 trainers in 1946 from Australia. The FB.VI were flown to New Zealand from Britain in an epic of aircraft delivery. Many of the

Above: A Czechoslovak Mosquito FB.Mk.VI (B-36), RF838, of the 24th Air Regiment. This particular aircraft was a combat veteran from World War Two, having flown with the RCAF's No.404 Squadron before being finally passed to Czechoslovakia in 1947 (Photo: via Lubomír Hodan).

surviving New Zealand Mosquitoes were sold off in 1956 at the end of their careers. Canadian-produced Mosquitoes were supplied to Britain during World War Two, although many Canadian-built Mosquitoes remained in Canada for Canadian service while some were supplied to the United States. Conversely, six British-built T.III trainers were supplied to Canada to help convert Canadian pilots onto the type who were to ferry Canadian-built Mosquitoes to Britain during the war. Australian-manufactured Mosquitoes were operated by the Royal Australian Air Force (RAAF), but British-supplied Mosquitoes were also flown by the RAAF. These included deliveries of the FB.VI in the A52-500 range, and No.1 Squadron, RAAF (coded NA), took the type into combat against the Japanese on the island of Borneo from its base on Labuan Island in July 1945. The RAAF also used the British-built PR.XVI, 23 being obtained in the A52-600 serial number range. The Mosquito remained in the RAAF inventory into the 1950's, and performed various tasks including a major aerial survey of Australia. The last RAAF Mosquitoes made their final operational flight on 29 August 1953.

Belgium – The Mosquito NF.Mk.30 was ordered by Belgium from existing British stocks in early 1947. 24 airworthy examples (MB 1 to MB 24) were eventually ordered. Fairey Aviation at Ringway overhauled the aircraft, with servicing in Belgium subsequently undertaken by the Belgian branch of Fairey at

Gosselies. Eight T.III were also obtained, numbered from MA 1, with one for ground instruction, plus at least two FB.VI, an NF.XVII and an NF.XIX. The NF.30 contingent served with two squadrons, Nos.10 and 11, of No.1 Wing of the Belgian air force (named the Force Aérienne Belge/Belgische Luchtmacht from early 1949), but problems with maintenance forced their grounding in 1953, although the last flight was in 1956. They were eventually replaced by Armstrong Whitworth Meteor NF.11 jet-powered night-fighters, the first of which was delivered in 1952.

China – Arguably the largest export operator of the Mosquito was China, which bought substantial numbers of Canadian-built Mosquitoes from Canada. These were ordered in 1947 for use by the Chinese Nationalist forces of Chiang Kai-shek, and eventually approximately 205 Mosquitoes were supplied. All were from Canadian production, and were shipped to Chinese Nationalist-held Shanghai. De Havilland personnel (technicians and pilots) from Canada were subsequently involved in preparing the Mosquitoes to be flown by Chinese pilots. Initial deliveries were made in February 1948, but by then the Chinese civil war was already going badly for the Chinese Nationalist forces. Most of the Mosquitoes subsequently delivered were of the FB.26 variety, but one T.22 and several T.27 trainers were also included to familiarise the Chinese pilots, who were more conversant with American types. No.3 Squadron of the Chinese Nationalist forces at Hankow definitely operated the Mosquito, and also possibly Nos. 1 and 4 squadrons, and the type saw much action against Chinese communist forces. The Canadian technicians left China in December 1948, and with the defeat of Chinese Nationalist forces some of the surviving Mosquitoes were evacuated to Formosa (today's Taiwan).

Czechoslovakia – a number of Czechoslovak pilots flew Mosquitoes with RAF squadrons during World War Two, including No.68 Squadron. Amongst them was the high-scoring Flt/Lt Karel Kuttelwasher (sometimes spelt Kuttelwascher in Czech, with at least 18 confirmed victories) of No.23 Squadron, although

Left: Publicity photo of Mosquito FB.VI A52-500 (a British-built aircraft) of No.1 Squadron, RAAF. Australian operations began with PR Mosquitoes in 1944, and 212 are known to have been built in Australia, plus some 76 supplied from Britain including a pattern aircraft (Photo: RAAF).

no specifically Czechoslovak-manned squadrons flew the type as their main equipment. However, when the Czechoslovak air force was reconstituted after the war, the Mosquito was ordered to equip at least one fighter-bomber squadron, with approximately 19 FB.VI being supplied from existing stocks (and called B-36 in Czech service), plus several T.III trainers (CB-36). Some of the deliveries were made in 1947, and at least two FB.VI were re-armed with German weapons. The fighter-bomber Mosquitoes initially served with a unit often referred to as the 'Atlantic Squadron'. However, with the reorganisation of the Czechoslovak air force along more Soviet lines in the later 1940's, they became a part of the 24th Air Regiment's first squadron (1.letka, LP 24 or letecký pluk 24, code letters IY) and second squadron (code letters JX), based at Plzen-Bory. This regiment was further reorganised in 1949 and the Mosquitoes were withdrawn with the arrival of Soviet types, some Mosquito aircrew later transitioning onto the Ilyushin Il-28 jet bomber.

Dominican Republic – six FB.Mk.VI were ordered post-war by this Caribbean nation, with deliveries commencing in 1948; serial numbers included '301'.

France – The most important export operator in Europe of the Mosquito was France, which received over 100 Mosquitoes of several marks including the NF.30, PR.XVI and some 57 FB.VI. Initial deliveries from British surplus stocks were made to the Armée de l'Air later in 1945, with the first squadron of the third French fighter wing GC I/3 'Corse' (GC = Groupe de Chasse or fighter wing) being formed on the FB.VI in November 1945. This squadron was renumbered as GC I/6 in November 1946, and was later joined by GC II/6 'Normandie-Niémen' also on the FB.VI. Both squadrons flew for a time from one of the French possessions in North Africa, but GC I/6 also spent some time from 1947 in French Indo-China, where the Mosquitoes were used in combat. The FB.VI was withdrawn from French service in July

Former Mosquito TR.Mk.33, serial number IDFAF 4x3186, from a batch of Mosquitoes supplied to the Israel Defence Force/Air Force in 1954-55. Amongst Israeli Mosquito squadrons, Nos.109 and 110 Squadrons flew former French Mosquitoes (Photo: MAP).

1949, but the NF.30 and PR.XVI continued in French service until June 1953. The French Mosquitoes retained their former British serial numbers, the PR.XVI reconnaissance aircraft being operated from 1945 to 1953, and the NF.30 night-fighters also until 1953; for a time they were included in a combined unit called I/31 'Lorraine', heir to the traditions of the former bomb group GB I/20 of wartime fame, based at Rabat-Salé in Morocco.

Israel – The exact number of Mosquitoes that found their way to Israel, either legitimately or by less scrupulous means, will probably never be known for certain. Without doubt the type proved to be very valuable to the Israelis in combat, and a number of marks were used by Israel including the FB.VI, PR.XVI, NF.30, former Royal Navy TR.33, and trainer T.III. The first delivery was of a PR.XVI, in July 1948. In early 1951 deals were made for the supply of up to 68 former French-operated Mosquitoes, which were delivered from June 1951. The surviving Israeli Mosquitoes were withdrawn prematurely in mid-1956, partly because some were becoming un-glued, but a number were returned for service in the Suez campaign later that year and served until 1958.

Norway – Mosquitoes were flown by Norwegian pilots as a part of the RAF during World War Two, the RAF's No.333 (Norwegian) Squadron being equipped with Mosquito FB.VI fighter-bombers from 1943. With the end of World War Two the 'B' Flight of this squadron was re-numbered with its Mosquitoes as No.334 Squadron and was deployed to Norway with its aircraft, coming under Royal Norwegian Air Force control in November 1945. Three T.III trainers and 10 additional FB.VI were later obtained from British surplus stocks, plus a B.25 for instructional purposes. Two of the FB.VI were later converted with radar added as makeshift night-fighters. However, a fatal accident in early 1951 led to all Norwegian

Mosquitoes being grounded, and they were removed from the inventory in January 1952.

Soviet Union – One Mosquito B.IV series II, DK296, was supplied to the Soviet Union in the spring of 1944. Flown by a Soviet ferry crew from Errol, Scotland, and eventually arriving at Vnukovo, Moscow in April of that year, the Mosquito was subsequently evaluated by the LII, the Soviet aviation flight test and research establishment, from 25 April to 15 May 1944. The aircraft was war-weary, a veteran of RAF operations with No.105 Squadron, and did not overly impress the Soviets, although there is some evidence that thought had been given to licence-producing or even copying the design in the Soviet Union. This ultimately did not happen, but Soviet records suggest that a complaint was made that no further Mosquitoes were supplied for evaluation. DK296 made a belly-landing on its ninth test flight in the Soviet Union and was not repaired.

Above: DK296 prior to delivery to the Soviet Union (Photo: British Aerospace).

Sweden – During 1948, 60 Mosquito NF.XIX were ordered for Swedish service from existing stocks. Deliveries began in July 1948, the aircraft being numbered from 30001 (formerly TA286) onwards. In Royal Swedish Air Force service the type was known as the J.30, and the aircraft served with that air force's F1 fighter wing - the Mosquito being the first real night fighter in Swedish service. The final Swedish-

Two Armée de l'Air Mosquitoes, with PR.Mk.XVI RF973 nearest the camera, formate near to what is believed to be the North African coastline. In French service the Mosquito operated from 1945 until 1953 (Photo: SHAA).

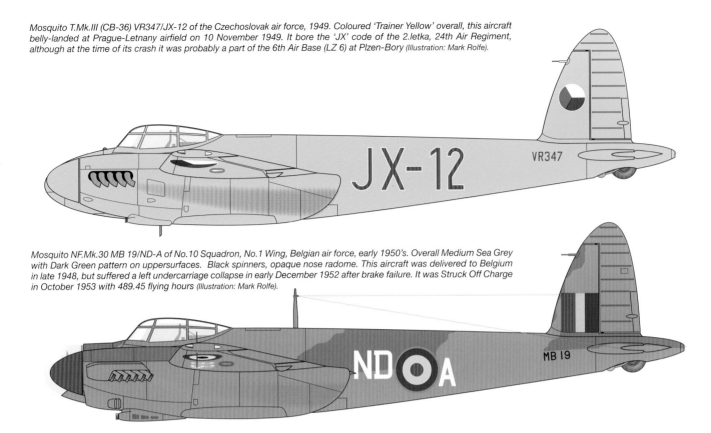

Mosquito T.Mk.III (CB-36) VR347/JX-12 of the Czechoslovak air force, 1949. Coloured 'Trainer Yellow' overall, this aircraft belly-landed at Prague-Letnany airfield on 10 November 1949. It bore the 'JX' code of the 2.letka, 24th Air Regiment, although at the time of its crash it was probably a part of the 6th Air Base (LZ 6) at Plzen-Bory (Illustration: Mark Rolfe).

Mosquito NF.Mk.30 MB 19/ND-A of No.10 Squadron, No.1 Wing, Belgian air force, early 1950's. Overall Medium Sea Grey with Dark Green pattern on uppersurfaces. Black spinners, opaque nose radome. This aircraft was delivered to Belgium in late 1948, but suffered a left undercarriage collapse in early December 1952 after brake failure. It was Struck Off Charge in October 1953 with 489.45 flying hours (Illustration: Mark Rolfe).

operated Mosquito made the type's last flight in March 1955, although the Swedish Mosquitoes had been removed from front-line service during the previous year, several accidents due to structural failure having taken place.

Switzerland – Two RAF Mosquitoes, PR.IV DK310 and FB.VI NS993, force-landed in Switzerland during World War Two (the former in August 1942 on an early Mosquito photo mission), and were retained by the Swiss authorities. DK310 was civil registered in Switzerland as HB-IMO for a time, and NS993 was used for trials by the Swiss armed forces' technical and trials establishment KTA. There it was fitted with an SM-1 jet engine (a Swiss development of the Armstrong Siddeley Mamba engine) in an installation below the fuselage for development purposes. Both these Swiss Mosquitoes were later scrapped.

Turkey – One of the largest post-war users of the Mosquito was Turkey, although the service details of the Turkish Mosquitoes are little known. At least 60 FB.VI are known to have been supplied, plus 10 T.III trainers, at least some of the latter being configured to carry bombs externally.

United States – Aside from Britain and the British Commonwealth, a major wartime user of the Mosquito was the US Army Air Force. American requests for Mosquitoes were made as early as 1942, and licence production in the US of the type was even considered. Eventually some two hundred Mosquitoes served with the US Army Air Force, especially in Britain where units of the Eighth Army Air Force flew Mosquitoes, principally on weather reconnaissance and other bomber support functions. The main version involved was the PR.XVI, all of

Although the majority of Mosquitoes that were used by the US Army Air Force during World War Two were from existing British stocks, 40 were made specially in Canada for American service under the designation F-8. Two F-8s, serial numbers 43-34928 and 43-34960, were flown from August 1944 by NACA at Langley, Virginia, for various test purposes - one of these is seen here (Photo: NASA).

which were supplied from production for the RAF, and the T.III trainer. Weather reconnaissance and chaff-dispensing Mosquitoes were flown from Watton, Norfolk, by the 653rd Bombardment Squadron of the 25th Bombardment Group (originally the provisional 802nd Reconnaissance Group up to August 1944). That unit's 654th BS also flew Mosquitoes for night photography and target radar-scope photography, the latter being specially-converted to carry H2X radar equipment. A handful of PR.XVI specially equipped to communicate with agents on the ground were also operated by the 654th BS under the code-name 'Red Stocking'. Approximately five T.III were also used by the Eighth Army Air Force, which employed at least 145 Mosquitoes in 1944-5. All survivors were returned to the RAF in the summer of 1945. In total, 40 Mosquitoes were supplied to the US from Canadian production under the designation F-8. Most were B.XX equivalents and therefore approximated to the B.IV, and were converted into reconnaissance aircraft by Bell at Buffalo, New York. The Americans found these aircraft to be lacking in performance, but some were trialled by the Army Air Force. Two served with NACA. Many were exchanged for the higher-performance PR.XVI. The USAAF also operated the Mosquito NF.30, the 416th Night Fighter Squadron in Italy flying the type from December 1944 until the end of the war.

Yugoslavia – The Yugoslav air force (JRV) was a major operator of the Mosquito between 1951 and 1963, the only communist-aligned air force to order and operate the type. A Yugoslav delegation visited Britain in 1951 and later placed orders for Mosquitoes that eventually totalled some 140 aircraft, including 60 NF.38, four T.III, and some 76 of the inevitable FB.VI. Deliveries began in 1951 but were spread over several years. All these aircraft were former RAF machines, but some were very late production and had been stored following completion. A number of the FB.VI were converted by the Yugoslavs into T.III dual-control trainers after delivery. Yugoslav Mosquitoes were numbered on the 8000 and 8100 numerical series. In Yugoslav service the Mosquitoes served with regiments of the 32nd Bombardment Division (FB.VI) and the 21st Mixed Aviation Division, the latter having a naval support role and some of whose Mosquitoes were configured to carry torpedoes. The 103rd Reconnaissance Regiment served as the JRV's Mosquito training and conversion facility, but the 184th Reconnaissance Regiment also operated Mosquitoes in a front-line capacity. The latter was the final Yugoslav operational regiment, giving up its last Mosquitoes in the summer of 1960, but some Yugoslav Mosquitoes continued in service in a second-line capacity mainly as target-towers until 1963 – the same year that Britain's final target-towing Mosquitoes were retired.

Specifications

During its production life the Mosquito went through a number of significant development stages, reflecting the growth potential of the initial design and the versatility of the basic Mosquito layout. Due to this, the type's specifications changed during production and development, particularly in terms of performance and weapons-carrying capability. Dimensionally, there were slight variations in length between many of the versions – although this is not reflected in the specifications quoted in many published sources. The later bomber versions, for example, were slightly longer than the initial versions due to the use of two-stage Merlin engines in slightly lengthened cowlings, while the fighter versions differed slightly in length due to their nose-mounted machine guns as opposed to the Perspex-nosed bomber versions. The type's wing span, however, remained fairly constant, with the obvious exception of the high-altitude developments with extended wingtips – for example the special Mk.XV high-altitude fighter development, and the PR.32 high-altitude reconnaissance version with a span of 59

ft 2 in (18 m). The most important early production Mosquito, the B.IV series II, included the following figures -

Specifications –	**de Havilland Mosquito B.Mk.IV series II**
Wingspan	54 ft 2 in (16.51 m)
Length	40 ft 9.5 in (12.43)
Maximum speed	385 mph (620 km/h) at 21,000 ft (6,400 m)
Maximum take-off weight	22,380 lb (10,152 kg)
Range	at least 1,220 miles (1,963 km)
Service ceiling	31,000 ft (9,449 m)
Armament	up to 2,000 lb (907 kg) of bombs, or 4,000 lb (1,814 kg) with fuselage modification for deeper bomb bay
Engine	Two Rolls-Royce Merlin 23 inline piston engines, of 1,390 hp each
Crew	Two

Mosquito Serial Numbers

The following is a comprehensive and extensively researched listing of the serial numbers allocated to each mark of Mosquito. As noted in the text, however, some aircraft from allotted batches of a particular version were occasionally completed to the standard of a different mark, or were used as prototypes or development aircraft for a later version - where possible in the following listing these have been included with the version that they were completed as.

British Production

Prototypes	W4050, W4051, W4052
F.Mk.II/T.Mk.III	W4053
PR.Mk.I	W4054-W4056, W4058-W4063 (and W4089)
PR.Mk.IV	W4066
B.Mk.IV series I	W4057, W4064-W4072
F.Mk.II/NF.Mk.II	W4074, W4076, W4078-W4088, W4090-W4099
T.Mk.III	W4073, W4075, W4077
NF.Mk.II	DD600-DD644, DD659-DD691, DD712-DD759, DD777-DD800, DZ228-DZ272, DZ286-DZ310, DZ653-DZ661, DZ680-DZ727, DZ739-DZ761, HJ642-HJ661, HJ699-HJ715, HJ911-HJ944
T.Mk.III	HJ851-HJ899, HJ958-HJ999, LR516-LR541, LR553-LR585, RR270-RR319, TV954-TV984, TW101-TW119, VA871-VA894, VA923-VA928, VR330-VR349, VT581-VT596, VT604-VT631
B.Mk.IV/PR.Mk.IV	DK284-DK303, DK308-DK333, DK336-DK339, DZ311-DZ320, DZ340-DZ341, DZ343-DZ388, DZ404-DZ442, DZ458-DZ497, DZ515-DZ559, DZ575-DZ618, DZ630-DZ652
FB.Mk.VI	HJ662-HJ682, HJ716-HJ743, HJ755-HJ792, HJ808-HJ833, HP848-HP888, HP904-HP942, HP967-HP989, HR113-HR162, HR175-HR220, HR236-HR262, HR279-HR312, HR331-HR375, HR387-HR415, HR432-HR465, HR485-HR527, HR539-HR580, HR603-HR648, HX802-HX835, HX851-HX869, HX896-HX901, HX905-HX922, HX937-HX984, LR248-LR276, LR289-LR313, LR327-LR340, LR343-LR389, LR402-LR404, MM398-MM423, MM426-MM431, NS819-NS859, NS873-NS914, NS926-NS965, NS977-NS999, NT112-NT156, NT169-NT199, NT201-NT207, NT219-NT223, NT226-NT238, PZ161-PZ203, PZ217-PZ250, PZ253-PZ259, PZ273-PZ299, PZ302-PZ316, PZ330-PZ358, PZ371-PZ419, PZ435-PZ466, PZ471-PZ476, RF580-RF625, RF639-RF681, RF695-RF736, RF749-RF793, RF818-RF859, RF873-RF915, RF928-RF966, RS501-RS535, RS548-RS580, RS593-RS633, RS637-RS680, RS693-RS698, SZ958-SZ999, TA113-TA122, TA369-TA388, TA469-TA508, TA523-TA560, TA575-TA603, TE587-TE628, TE640-TE669, TE683-TE725, TE738-TE780, TE793-TE830, TE848-TE889, TE905-TE932, VL726-VL732
PR.Mk.VIII	conversions from Mk.IV inc. DK324, DZ343, DZ364, DZ404, DZ424
PR.Mk.IX	LR405-LR446, LR459-LR474, LR478-LR481, MM227-MM236, MM239-MM240, MM242-MM257
B.Mk.IX	LR475-LR477, LR495-LR513, ML896-ML924, MM237-MM238, MM241
NF.Mk.XII	HJ945-HJ946, HK107-HK141, HK159-HK204, HK222-HK236
NF.Mk.XIII	HK363-HK382, HK396-HK437, HK453-HK481, HK499-HK536, MM436-MM479, MM491-MM534, MM547-MM590, MM615-MM623
NF.Mk.XV	MP469, conversions included DZ366, DZ385, DZ409, DZ417
B./PR.Mk.XVI	ML896-ML920, ML925-ML942, ML956-ML999, MM112-MM156, MM169-MM205, MM219-MM226, PF379-PF415, PF428-PF469, PF481-PF526, PF538-PF579, PF592-PF619, RV295-RV326, RV340-RV363, TA614-TA616

PR.Mk.XVI	DZ540, MM258, MM271-MM314, MM327-MM371, MM384-MM397, NS496-NS538, NS551-NS596, NS619-NS660, NS673-NS712, NS725-NS758, NS772-NS816, RF969-RF999, RG113-RG158, RG171-RG175
NF.Mk.XVII	HK237-HK265, HK278-HK327, HK344-HK362
FB.Mk.XVIII	including HJ732, HX902-HX904, MM424-MM425, NT200, NT224-NT225, NT592-NT593, PZ251-PZ252, PZ300-PZ301, PZ346, PZ467-PZ470
NF.Mk.XIX	MM624-MM656, MM669-MM685, TA123-TA156, TA169-TA198, TA215-TA249, TA263-TA308, TA323-TA357, TA389-TA357, TA389-TA413, TA425-TA449
NF.Mk.30	MM686-MM710, MM726-MM769, MM783-MM822, MT456-MT500, MV521-MV570, NT241-NT283, NT295-NT336, NT349-NT393, NT415-NT458, NT471-NT513, NT526-NT568, NT582-NT621, RK929-RK954
PR.Mk.32	MM328, conversions included NS582, NS586-NS589
TF/TR.Mk.33	LR359, LR387, TS444, TS449, TW227-TW257, TW277-TW295
PR.Mk.34	PF620-PF635, PF647-PF680, RG176-RG215, RG228-RG269, RG283-RG318, VL613-VL625
B.Mk.35	RS699-RS723, RV364-RV367, TA617-TA618, TA633-TA670, TA685-TA724, RV364-RV367, TA617-TA618, TA633-TA670, TA685-TA724, TH977-TH999, TJ113-TJ158, TK591-TK635, TK648-TK656, VP178-VP202, VR792-VR806
NF.Mk.36	RK955-RK960, RK972-RK999, RL113-RL158, RL173-RL215, RL229-RL268
TF./TR.Mk.37	VT724-VT737
NF.Mk.38	VT651-VT683, VT691-VT707, VX860-VX879, VX886-VX916

Canadian Production

B.Mk.VII	KB300-KB324
F-8	43-34924 to 43-34963 (for USAAF)
B.Mk.XX	KB100-KB299, KB325-KB369
FB.Mk.21	KA100-KA102
T.Mk.22	KA873-KA876, KA896-KA897
B.Mk.25	KA930-KA999, KB370-KB699
FB.Mk.26	KA103-KA450 (some cancelled, others as T.29)
T.Mk.27	KA877-KA895, KA898-KA927
T.Mk.29	several between KA117-KA314

Australian Production

FB.Mk.40	A52-1 to A52-212 (but not all finished as FB.40)
PR.Mk.40	conversions included A52-2, A52-4, A52-6, A52-7 A52-9 and A52-26
PR.Mk.41	A52-300 to A52-327 (re-numbered from within FB.40 allocation)
T.Mk.43	A52-1050 to A52-1071 (re-numbered from within FB.40 allocation)

Mosquito Modelling

The Mosquito is one of the most popular modelling subjects, and over the years a very large number of Mosquito kits, accessories and decals have been produced in several scales by a wide range of manufacturers. It is impossible to list all of them here, particularly as some of these are long out of production and are no longer generally available. Listed below are the manufacturers who in early 2008 included Mosquito items in their ranges, although it must be stressed that availability is dependant upon many factors and some items are unavailable in some countries. One of the best sources of information on currently-available items is the British model shop Hannants (www.hannants.co.uk) which carries stock of many of the manufacturers listed here, and can perform world-wide mail order.

KITS

Airfix	1:72	Mosquito NF.Mk.II/ FB.Mk.VI/XVIII
Airfix	1:72	Mosquito NF.Mk.XIX/J.30
Airfix	1:48	Mosquito FB.Mk.VI
Airfix	1:48	Mosquito NF.Mk.30
Airfix	1:48	Mosquito B.Mk.XVI/ PR.Mk.XVI
Hasegawa	1:72	Mosquito FB.Mk.VI
Tamiya	1:72	Mosquito FB.Mk.VI/ NF.Mk.II
Tamiya	1:72	Mosquito B.Mk.IV/ PR.Mk.IV
Tamiya	1:72	Mosquito NF.Mk.XIII/XVII
Tamiya	1:48	Mosquito FB.Mk.VI/ NF.Mk.II
Tamiya	1:48	Mosquito B.Mk.IV/ PR.Mk.IV
Tamiya	1:48	Mosquito NF.Mk.XIII/XVII

www.airfix.com   www.tamiya.com
www.hasegawa-model.co.jp

TRANSFERS/DECALS

AeroMaster	48
Carpena	72/48
Cutting Edge	72/48
Kits at War	72/48
Eagle Strike	72/48
MPD/Mini Print	72
RAF Dec	72
Tally Ho	72/48
Ventura	72/48/32
Xtradecal	72/48

ACCESSORIES
(detail parts, conversions, canopies, etc)

Aeroclub Models	72
Airwaves	72
Aires	72/48
Cutting Edge	48
Czech Master	72/48
Eduard	72/48
Falcon	72/48
Hi Tech	48
Magna Models	72
Paragon Designs	72/48
Pavla Models	72
Quickboost	72/48
Squadron Signal	72/48
True Details	72/48
Verlinden Productions	48

Note –
72 = 1:72 scale, 48 = 1:48 scale, etc.

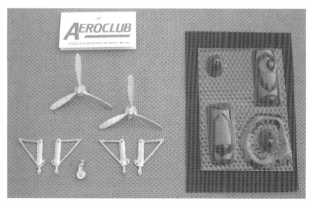

Aeroclub Models 1/72 scale Mosquito accessories inc. canopies, propellers, and undercarriage components.

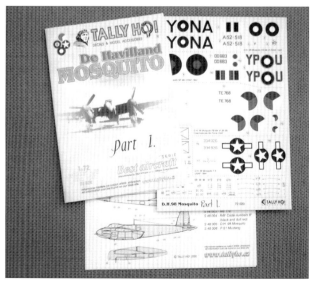

Tally Ho 1/72 scale Mosquito decals.

Further Details

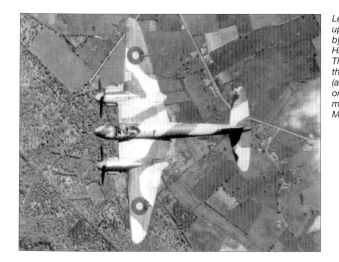

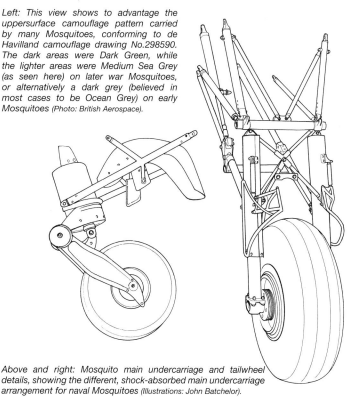

Left: This view shows to advantage the uppersurface camouflage pattern carried by many Mosquitoes, conforming to de Havilland camouflage drawing No.298590. The dark areas were Dark Green, while the lighter areas were Medium Sea Grey (as seen here) on later war Mosquitoes, or alternatively a dark grey (believed in most cases to be Ocean Grey) on early Mosquitoes (Photo: British Aerospace).

Above and right: Mosquito main undercarriage and tailwheel details, showing the different, shock-absorbed main undercarriage arrangement for naval Mosquitoes (Illustrations: John Batchelor).

Left: The Mosquito often made use of external fuel tanks, these were available in 3 sizes as seen here: 50, 100 and 200 Imperial gallons (Photo: HSA).

Preserved Mosquitoes

At the time of writing (early 2008), there were seven complete Mosquitoes on public display or under active restoration for display in museums in Britain, in addition to several additional on-going restoration projects and incomplete airframes. The seven preserved aircraft, including the priceless prototype, are as follows –

de Havilland Aircraft Heritage Centre
(incorporating the **Mosquito Aircraft Museum**),
London Colney, Hertfordshire
www.dehavillandmuseum.co.uk
W4050   Prototype
TA122   FB.Mk.VI
TA634   TT.Mk.35

RAF Museum Cosford, Cosford, Shifnal,Shropshire
www.rafmuseum.org.uk/cosford
TA639   TT.Mk.35

RAF Museum Hendon, north London
www.rafmuseum.org.uk/london
TJ138   B.Mk.35

Yorkshire Air Museum, Elvington, York
www.yorkshireairmuseum.co.uk
HJ711   NF.Mk.II

Imperial War Museum, Duxford Airfield,
Cambridgeshire
http://duxford.iwm.org.uk
TA719   TT.Mk.35

Several other Mosquitoes exist in other parts of the world, the most readily accessible for British readers being the unique NF.Mk.30 RK952 in the Musée Royal de l'Armée et d'Histoire Militaire in Brussels, Belgium (www.klm-mra.be)

Internet Resources: In addition to the above websites, an excellent web resource for Mosquito information, updates and a useful forum is www.mossie.org. Also useful is: www.dhmosquito.com.

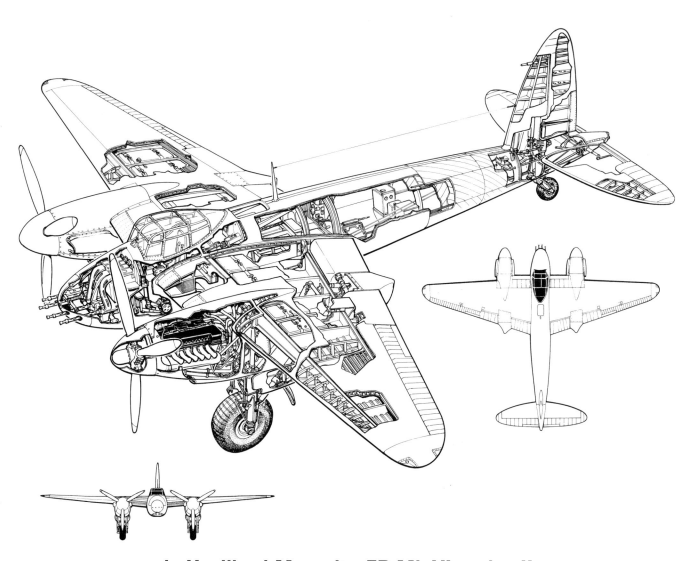

de Havilland Mosquito FB.Mk.VI series II

Mosquito NF.Mk.38, VT653, was one of a batch of 50 (serial numbers VT651 to VT683, VT691 to VT707) of this late mark of night-fighter Mosquito that were built by de Havilland, several from this batch later being transferred to Yugoslavia. Note the aircraft's two-stage Merlin engines, virtually clear nose radome and unusual partly unpainted (primer?) finish (Photo: HSA).